# IDEAS
# FOR
# NAUGHTY FUN
## *Extended Edition*

By: Tim A. Rowland

I0439469

The naughty ideas found in this book are the product of my experiences, imagination, concepts created while writing erotica and romance novels, and more than a few other sources. Some of these will be widely known and many are rather original; born of my own mind. I would like to say up front though that you should always use caution and a clear head when trying to attempt any of these ideas. I am merely giving you the concepts…what you do with them and your health and safety are on you. Stay safe, stay healthy, and stay to have fun another day. Now that we have cleared that up, let's talk about what you are going to find in this book.

This book contains ideas for parties, naughty games, and so much more. One thing you should keep in mind is that the ideas found in this book are anywhere from an "R" rating…all the way to an "XXX" rating or so. You won't have any warning as to the rating either… it can go from one extreme to the other. You might be asking why I did that; well, the answer is simple; if you are old enough to read the book then you are old enough to have no need of being protected from sudden extreme adult content. Am I right? Of course I am. The ideas are simply written and formatted in plain English.

Enjoy ☺
Play safe,
play smart…
but play often!

Remember the book I told you about a moment ago? It is called "Naughty Ways to Play Normal Games" and is also available on Amazon and Kindle…but you get it right here and right now. It is a guidebook that gives you the idea, concept, and a few other fast facts about ways that you can turn very normal games in to very naughty (and much more fun) games. We will start there…then move on to some classic and traditional ideas…and the come the ones you probably never thought of ☺

### *** PLEASE NOTE ***

This book mentions many games & other products made by various companies. The author in no way claims any ownership or any other type of connection with the makers of these games. Games mentioned in this book are the sole property of their creators. This book in no way means to infringe on the copyright or image of these products or the companies which create and/or sell the products.

Also, the games found in this book are the ideas and creative thoughts of one man.  Please be sure to use caution and common sense when attempting to take part in any game mentioned in this book.  The author is in no way responsible for how, when, or where you choose to play the games described here.  This book is for entertainment purposes and is not intended to be a manual.  Play and re-create these games at your own will and at your own risk.  You are responsible for your actions…not me. ☺

- Please check the back of the book for content locations.
- This book is intended for adults only and contains language and content that is not suitable for those under the legal age of sexual consent in your country and area.

Thank you,
    Tim A. Rowland

# STRIP UNO

- This one is very simple to understand.
    - Get either 1 or 2 packs of Uno cards, depending on how many players there will be.
    - Play the game just as you normally would; according to the directions included in the pack of cards.

Since many people play by different rules I will specify that if you do not have the color or face card needed for your turn, only draw one card from the deck. If you are still unable to lay down a card, it is simply the next person's turn.

## PLAY IT EITHER OF THESE WAYS:

- When a player runs out of cards, all the other players must strip one article of clothing.

    Or

- When a player runs out of cards, the player left holding the most amount (or highest total  point value) of cards must strip one article of clothing.

    Cards' Values:

- Number cards are worth the face value number.
- Skips are worth 20 points.
- Draw Twos are worth 50 points.
- Reverses are worth 20 points.
- Wild Cards are worth 100 points.
- Draw Fours are worth 200 points.

# <u>TRUTH OR DARE</u>

- Everyone knows how to play this… if you don't… ask any random stranger and they can probably tell you lol.

  Our Twist Begins….

- If you choose truth and don't want to answer the question, you can remove an article of clothing instead.
- If you are caught lying to a "truth" question, you must remove 2 articles of clothing.
- Players decide what happens if a dare is not done. Decide before the game starts how or what the punishment would be.

  GOOD GENERAL RULES:

- No dares which are almost certain to get the person arrested.
- No dares which are almost certain to cause long lasting danger or issues to anyone.

# STRIP PONG

- This is a variation on the classic "beer pong" and is very easy to understand. Set up 10 cups full of any liquid (since it's not actually beer pong, don't waste the beer lol) and place them in a triangle formation on one side of the table. Do the same on the other side of the table.
- One team stands at each end of the table (usually guys on one side and girls on the other... or one couple on each end).
- Use a ping pong ball or golf ball (any small ball that bounces will work really) and try to bounce the ball off of the table and into one of the cups in front of the opposite team. The ball must bounce off something (usually the table) at least once before going into the cup.
- If someone gets the ball in your team's cup, your member must remove one article of clothing (or switch so that your team alternates who takes something off).
- If the ball lands in a cup, remove that cup from the table. Then rearrange the remaining cups into a smaller formation before your team takes their turn.

NOTE: You may also want to try playing with the cups arranged in a circle or X instead of a triangle formation.

# STRIP TWISTER

- Another very simple to understand and play kind of game. Well, easy for some ☺
- Play the game just as the included directions (in the box) indicate, by spinning the dial (or rolling dice depending on which version of Twister you are playing) and then follow what it says.
- Simply put…you fall… you take something off.


ADDED CHALLENGE:   Add baby oil, massage oil, or even Astroglide to the mat.

- Try to limit the number of people on the mat at one time. If the number of players causes the game to be a danger to anyone, please invest in purchasing another mat to connect via tape or a heavy item so that the playing field is expanded. Safety above all else!!

# I NEVER

- The players gather and starting from one side of the room, the first player (far right or far left) thinks of something they have never done (make it fun and naughty) and simply says, "I never_____."
- Anyone who has done what is says, removes an article of clothing.

  OR

- Mix this with the original version of this game (drinking game) and simply add the rule that anyone who has to take a drink 3 (or however many) times in a row has to remove an article of clothing.

  OR

- Each player writes down as many things as they can remember ever doing (make is naughty) onto a small piece of paper.
- Fold all the pieces of paper in two and place them into a bowl or large container.
- Mix them up really well.

- Take turns drawing out a piece of paper from the container (individual or a member of your team) and if you have done what is written on the paper, you must remove an article of clothing.

# CHANCE

(Fast Version)

- Get as many decks of playing cards as needed allowing each player to have a large stack.  Leave the jokers in the deck(s).
- Divide the cards evenly among the players, face down.  Each player then stacks their cards in front of them still face down.
- Each person places their top card in the middle of the group, face up.
- The player with the lowest value card must remove an article of clothing.
- Number cards go by their face value.
- The face cards from lowest to highest are: jack, queen, king, ace.
- The joker card is an automatic lose.  If more than one player places down a joker at the same time… both players lost and must remove an article of clothing.

*** A second round can then be played using sexual acts in place of clothes for the loser of that hand/round. ***

(Slow Version)

- This version is set up ready to play the same as the fast version.
- Once all players are ready with their decks in front of them face down, each player places their top card in the middle, face up.
- The player with the highest card then collects all of the cards played for that hand.
- After everyone has played the last card in their pile, the person with the least amount of cards...
    - Takes off an article of clothing
    - Or plays naked for the remainder of the game and this is repeated until only one person is left with any clothes on.
- If two players play the same face value card in the same hand, and it is the lowest card played, then the group will decide (before the game starts) if both players strip or if they play another card to determine a lowest (this can cause those persons to run out of cards before the others though).

(Dice Version)

- This game can also be played with dice by simply having each player roll the dice (however many you want) and writing down the person's roll total.
- In this version if two players roll the same number, and it is the lowest number rolled, they must each roll again to determine a lowest.

# SNAPS

- Gather a large number of rubber bands of several different colors.
- Each player places a rubber band on their wrist that represents the act they are willing to do.
- You can make up your own chart or follow this guideline:
  Green rubber band is a kiss
  Blue rubber band is finger her
  White rubber band is a blow job
  Black rubber band means intercourse
  Orange rubber band means eat her out.
  …etc
- If someone snaps the rubber band, you must do what that color represents.

- Each act must be represented specifically. Such as, "blowjob" & "eating out" must be 2 different colors instead of just saying a certain color is oral sex.
  This is to prevent any confusion during games involving players who are bisexual or homosexual.

# GROUP CHOICE CHALLENGES
## A.K.A "I DARE YOU" or "I BET YOU WON'T"

- All the players choose "whatever number decided" amount of ideas for people to do as challenges. Write each one on a separate piece of paper. Fold each piece of paper in half.
- Place all of the pieces of paper with the challenges on them in a bowl, hat, or other container.

WAYS TO DO THIS:
- Draw a card off a random deck and the person who draws the lowest number must pick a challenge to do.
- Just take turns picking a challenge to do from the collection.
- Make a rule that anyone who does or says "____" has to pick a challenge and do it. (for parties mostly)
  - The more creative the minds in the group, the more fun and challenging this can be.
- Good examples of challenges would be:
  - Strip Tease
  - Flash in Public
  - Masturbate in the Local Library (Borderline)

- Unless agreed on beforehand you are not allowed to write a challenge that forces anyone to do something to you. Such as "Give (your name) a blowjob" or anything of that sort.
- Also you may not write a challenge that is sure to get someone arrested or physically harmed.

The group/players can decide (before the game starts) what happens if the challenge is not done. A good rule is the player must pick 2 challenges and do both.

# NAUGHTY EASTER HUNT

- Obviously, if it is not Easter then you will need to have saved material from earlier, or find a substitute for the Easter eggs.
- Purchase plastic Easter eggs made for hiding candy inside. Buy two separate colors. (Blue & Pink)
- Write naughty acts on little pieces of paper and place one in each egg.
- The man (or men) will hunt for one color and the woman (or women) will hunt for the other.
- If playing with several players then specify on the paper who the naughty act will be done by/with.

# NAUGHTY MARCO POLO

- Decide on a playing field such as a large room or the entire house. If you can get away with a much larger area such as a large yard that allows for total privacy then all the better.
- Both (or all) players begin the game already naked.
- If the situation does not allow total darkness with the lights shut off, then blind fold the person chosen to go first.
- The other player(s) after the chosen person can no longer see will spread out within the playing field.
- Give a count that allows for the other players to spread out far enough (count should be based on the size of the playing field.)
- The chosen person then wanders around the playing field repeatedly saying "Marco" and the other players must immediately respond with "Polo."
- Each time the chosen person catches another player by tagging them an action is done. The action done should be progressive. Example:
  - First time caught you kiss the chosen person.

- o Second time caught you allow for a naughty feel.
- o Third time caught you please them with your hand.
- o Etc…
- Each time a player is caught and the action is done, they must be given no less than a count of 30 seconds to move off into another direction before the chosen person begins moving around and repeating "Marco."
  **----THAT'S IT----**

# NAUGHTY HANG MAN

- Draw on a piece of paper:
  - Straight line across (short)
  - Another short line up and down in the center of the previous line.
  - A short line across extending from the top of the vertical line.
  - A final short line coming down at the end of the horizontal line up top.
- Think of a word or short phrase for the other player(s) to guess.
- Under the picture place a single short line for each letter. Be sure to separate it so that the words can be easily determined. Example: The phrase "The Dog" would look like this "_ _ _ _ _ _."
- Play either of these two ways:
  - Each time a correct letter is guessed, write the letter where it goes in the phrase or word and take off one article of clothing.
  - Wait until the entire word or phrase is guessed and strip naked.
- Once you are naked, you sit down and another player comes up to create a word or phrase to be guessed. Keep your clothes off.

- Either way it is played, if a wrong letter is guessed, then a body part of a stick figure is placed hanging. Under the top line facing down to the wider base.
- If an entire man with head, body, arms, and legs is drawn then the person(s) guessing loses and you are safe.

# THE DICE DECIDE

- Each player writes 1-6 down a sheet a paper.
- For each number, assign an action you would like to have another player do to you.
- Each player rolls the dice.
- PLAYERS:
    - Couple (2 players) - You must do what the other player has assigned to that number.
    - Group (3+ players) - You must do what the next eligible person going clockwise has assigned to that number. Your next roll, you move to the next eligible person.
- Eligible means the next person who matches your sexual preference.
- As tempting as it may be, try to avoid putting "intercourse" or anything with the same meaning on your list for the first round. You can always write a new list later in the game and begin again. It is best if you make 3 or more lists and change each time the sequence of people starts over.

# NAUGHTY
# OR
# STRIP
# BLACK JACK

- One person acts as "dealer" or "the house."
- Place the entire deck of cards face down (of course shuffle them if it is a new deck).
- Flip the top card over so that it is face up (dealer's job). One card is flipped over in front of the opposite player and then one is flipped in front of the dealer.
- The opposite player (non-dealer) either picks "stay" or "hit." Stay means you keep what you have and hit means that another card is flipped over for that player.
- Player with the total card value closest to 21 wins.
  - Ace = 1 or 11
  - Face Card (king, queen, etc) = 10
  - All Other Cards = Number on Card.
- If a player goes over 21 then they bust and automatically lose.
- The losing player(s) must remove one article of clothing.

- Continue until only one player is wearing anything.

As many rounds as you want can be played…get creative with what must be done when a player loses.

# NAUGHTY OR STRIP HIDE & SEEK PLUS TAG

- Most know this one lol
- Pick one person to be "it."
- Agree on a range of space as the playing field.
- The chosen person closes their eyes and counts to 20 (or any high number).
- Everyone else scatters and hides.
- If the chosen person finds you and tags you, then you must remove an article of clothing.
- First person found and tagged is the next person to count and try to find the others.
- Once you lose the last article of clothing, you are out of the game.  However, you cannot put any clothes back on until the entire game is finished.
- Last player left wearing an article of clothing… WINS!!

This game is even more fun played in the rain.  Be sure there is <u>no lightning</u> though for safety.

# <u>NAUGHTY SCAVENGER HUNT</u>

- All players agree on a playing field.  This can be as confined as your house, or as wide as the city you live in…or larger.
- One player hides somewhere within the playing field.
- Spread clues around the game area.
- With each clue you leave an article of clothing.
- At the end of the hunt the winner(s) will find you naked.
- YOU DECIDE WHAT HAPPENS AT THAT POINT.

Please be sure if you make your playing field larger than your own home, that you:
- Hide the clues very well so that only the players will find them.
- Hide in a place such as a motel room or a very secluded spot.
- The idea is… don't get arrested or place yourself in danger.

# STRIP PHASE 10

- Play the game according to the normal rules and guidelines (included in the deck of cards)
- Anyone who hasn't gotten their phase once a player lays down their last card removes an article of clothing.
- Once a player has removed their last article of clothing, they may do dares or acts if their phase is not met, or they are out of the game.
- No player is allowed to put an article of clothing back on or cover up with any other item (blanket, towel, etc) until the game is entirely finished and one winner is determined.

# STRIP DARTS

- Unlike regular darts, you don't keep score in this version.
- Each player throws one dart at the dart board.
- Begin a small distance from the board.
- The player who gets their dart to stick in the board closest to the center red dot (bull's eye) wins.
- The player furthest from the center red dot must remove an article of clothing.
- If a dart is thrown and it does not stick into the board, that is an automatic loss.
- After each throw both players must move further from the board before attempting another throw.

# STRIP POOL

- Rack the pool balls on one end of the pool table. Shaped in a triangle. Be sure the "1" ball is in front and the "8" ball is in the middle.
- One player breaks by shooting the cue ball (white ball) into the triangle causing the balls to scatter around the table.
- The type of the first ball you sink into a pocket (striped or solid color) becomes your pool balls for the game.
- Sink all of your pool balls into the pockets; saving the "8" ball for last.
- If the "8" ball is sank by any player before all of your pool balls are off the table, then you automatically lose the game.
- Loser of each game must strip an article of clothing.
    - If you want to make the fun and game go faster, then a player must strip an article of clothing anytime a member of the opposite team sinks a ball.
- Teams can be used, but only one player may shoot at a time. If you choose to use two cue balls and allow two players from a team to shoot at the same time (just to be different)…then the stakes of the game should be raised as well.

# HIGHER or LOWER

- Choose one player to be the dealer.
- The dealer shuffles the cards (face down) and then flips the top 5-7 (your choice) cards face up in a line in front of them where all the players can see.
- Each player other than the dealer must guess if the next card to be placed on top of it will be higher or lower.
- For each incorrect guess, one article of clothing is removed by the guessing player(s).
- For each correct guess, one article of clothing is removed by the dealer.

If there are 4+ players, it is best to use two decks of cards and assign two dealers. Play as two separate games played side by side to each other. An alternative would be to play in teams. The dealer team takes turns dealing and the guessing team must agree on "lower" or "higher" each turn.

# MATCH UP

- Determine how many decks of cards to use based on the number of players. Approximately one deck for every 3 players. For obvious reasons you should use cards that are the same color and pattern on the backside. No cheating lol.
- Lay all the cards out in a square or circle pattern face down.
- Each player chooses two cards and tries to get two of the same card.
  - If using poker cards you can do same number only or require that the number and suit match.
  - If using Uno cards (or similar) than you can do face value only or face value and color match.
- Once a player gets to matching cards, they discard those cards and choose a player. The player they chose then removes one article of clothing.
- If two un-matching cards are picked up, then those cards must be returned to the position in the layout in which they came.

- Once a player is fully nude, they must remain nude until the game has ended and a winner is determined. That person is now out of the game unless it is agreed that "other" consequences result in place of the loss of clothing.

# Toga Party

As I said, we will start with the classics and traditional ideas. I'm sure everyone agrees that the toga party is the all-time classic and traditional idea. Toga parties have been around for years and years and enjoyed by countless numbers of generations, there is no doubt. Most people know the concept for this one; since it's pretty much a two-step thing. Traditionally the idea is everyone dresses in a toga (yes, like the romans) and then goes to the party somewhere. Like I said, two steps only. Well, why not make yours a little different and yes…complicated.

Make it a real 'Roman Toga Party' and have people decide if they want to attend as a Roman noble or a roman slave. You can run with this concept for as far as you wish. Maybe even have someone who wants to come as a Roman who owns gladiators…then have a few friends come as that person's gladiators. Others may want to dress as slaves and have friends (or boyfriend or girlfriend) dress as the master. Try to even set up Roman bath areas and things that would actually be found in that time period.

### Character Ideas:
Roman King
Roman Queen
Master
Slave

Gladiator
Peasant
Slave Trader
Roman Prisoner

Hold games like the real Romans did. Use your imagination…the more you use it, the better the event will be. Want to make it really naughty? Most slaves didn't wear clothes back then unless they were house slaves. Run wild.

# Wet Down Wars

The "Wet down wars" is a combination of two things you loved doing during hot weather as a kid…only way more fun as an adult. Water balloons and squirt guns…need I say more? Probably not, but I guess I will anyway. Get as large of a group of people as you can… preferably a large group of people you know very well. Bring your arsenal of squirt guns and balloons to the party. Have some available but like an army they can also supply better weapons for battle.

You can break into teams or you can make it a last person standing competition. You can be traditional and use water, but I would suggest using something more fun. A great idea (though it's expensive) is to use milk….very, very cold milk. Another option that is a little more cost effective is to mix either shaving cream or whip cream with hot water and then let the water cool off before shooting anyone with it.

The trouble with this is that it may cause damage or clogs in some squirt guns. I have no doubt that you are already thinking this yourself, but I would highly recommend getting a super soaker for this war. Now, you have your rifles and side arms...but don't forget the grenades (water balloons) and it is also always a good idea to set traps whenever possible. Remember, the balloons can be filled with straight shaving cream or whip cream, since the popping will splatter the contents everywhere anyway.

Surely you have figured out the concept of how to play this as a naughty game, but I will spell it out for you just in case. Each team or person gathers their arsenal and heads off (for added challenge when playing teams start by letting the other team hide your weapons and you hide theirs) and if you are sprayed or caught by a balloon from another player, you must take something off (maybe even what gets hit) until you are fully naked. Forget the gung ho attitude of no prisoners too... if someone is rendered fully nude... they become the other team's prisoner of war.

If you are a swinger kind of group…
then by all means even treat them like a prisoner
and do what you will with them.  Maybe even
use your squirt gun to hold them at gun point
and make a deal.  Trade a little attention for not
making them lose more clothes.  Be careful
though… others are still out to get you too.

One beauty of this game is that it doesn't
matter if there are 2 of you or 200 of you… it's
played the same and it's still a great time!

Be creative and have fun!

# You Got It… Flaunt It!

There is at least a little bit of an exhibitionist in each and every one of us. Some of us hide it and some of us show it to the world (no pun intended) any chance we can. The idea I'm about to suggest to you is great because you get to have fun… you'll make money at it too. No, you won't get to quit your day job (some might actually) but you could make some extra cash at the same time you are having fun. Do it for the fun and excitement though…not for the extra cash. I'm sure a lot of readers have probably already figured out what this page is about and what the suggestion/idea is, but again… I'm going to tell you anyway.

A great way to show off what you got and to feel the excitement of being an exhibitionist without having to see or watch the people who are watching you is broadcast on a cam site. Also, many of these sites will allow you to block states from viewing your bio and broadcast so that you can know that nobody you know will be watching you. If you want someone you know to see you on webcam, then just don't block any states or countries; maybe even send people there to watch.

Pretty much all of these web sites allow people to tip you in exchange for making a request, reaching a goal you set, or getting pictures/videos you put up to be available… which is how you can make money. Now, some people do use these sites as their full time job, but like I said before it is way better if you do it just for the thrill and naughty of it. There are tons of web sites that you can broadcast on and the ones I've ever seen are all pretty good. The one I would suggest using for the thrill of it and just to be naughty is one called **Chaturbate**. I suggest this one because you don't have to invest anything at all to broadcast on this site whenever you want. Most sites you have to have a premium account or you have to have already spent a certain amount of money before they will let you become a broadcaster on there.

With **Chaturbate**, you just sign up free and then send two pictures one of you and one of you holding your driver's license so they can prove you are of legal age. After that you are verified and you can have it. As long as you don't drink on camera or do anything illegal you are fine. You can even create several accounts if you want and use the same material to get verified for each of them. While you are there… check out some other people's cams too (when you are not broadcasting) and have fun with that too. In fact, you can use any tips you get to tip other people instead of buying some of your own.

Another great one and one that is maybe even larger and more well-known is **MyFreeCams**, but you have to buy tokens and become a premium member before you can broadcast yourself on there. Their rules seem a little more relaxed, but if you are looking to have some naughty fun without paying anything, then this one's not for you.

Have fun and I hope you get all the adoring fans you want ☺

## Lights, Cameras, & Some Action

This is another one of those that may be considered a classic and popular, but it will forever be worth mentioning as a naughty idea. Get a camera and as many people as you want… then have your own photo shoot. People think that it takes an expensive camera and a lot of props for your naughty pictures to come out looking decent. That's not true at all; in fact, you just need a camera (preferably digital) and a place to take them. If you want to use back drops, then go to your closet (or even your bed) and get different colored and patterns of sheets and blankets. After that, you get some push pins or really strong tape and mount the color or pattern you want to use to the wall or over a rail or anywhere you want to put it. You have just made an instant back drop.

Want to use props? Well, look around and I bet you find at least 20 or 30 things in and around your house that would make great props for photo shoots. Don't just use the furniture as props, use the little stuff you pass by every day and maybe even go outside and find nature provided props. Also, if you have the space then take some outside…as long as you can do it without getting arrested, then why wouldn't you?

Okay… what about things to model in, right?  Well, raid your closet and boxes and use what you already have.  Maybe if you can afford it, then buy or order some things to use.  Women have the advantage as models because they can raid their own closet and any man's closet and find things they can make sexy on them.  Also keep in mind that most all cameras have a timer function on them…by all means just set the camera up on a timer and then both of you get in the picture together.

As always… just be creative and have fun.

# Through the Day Word Game

This is probably the easiest to do and easiest to understand yet. This is another one of those that is more fun when there are more people; which makes it good for parties that involve friends (or lovers) who have known each other for a long time. Basically, you pick however many words you want. Try to pick a small amount of words though, but are both random and commonly used.

Anytime one of the words chosen (write them down so no one can claim it wasn't one of them) is said or heard in a song or on television or in any way... someone calls it and either: Everyone takes something off if said on the radio or television; or the person who says the word must take something off. What makes this game even more fun and even more challenging depends on the words you choose.

If it is just you and your special someone... then you may want to make it so that if you say the chosen words you have to do something naughty right up front. I keep saying it, but only because it always remains true... imagination will determine the level of fun you have... so be creative!

*See Next Page for Word Suggestions*

# <u>Great Words to Use:</u>

- What
- Dude
- Hey
- Hell
- Text
- Shit
- Why
- Huh (hmm counts too)

# It's All Just a Theme

Just like the toga party idea…always use attention to detail and get as in depth with the theme as you can possibly manage and afford to pull off, but rather than go through the whole thing again I thought I would just give you a quick list of other great themes to use for parties and roleplaying of all kinds. So here it is:

- Pimps & Hoes
- Medieval Times
- Colonial Times
- Hot Nerds, Geeks, and Dorks (If you are one of these…all the better)
- Pirates and Wenches
- Strippers & Chippendales
- Wild Animals & Hunters (Type "animal tail anal plug" into Amazon…see what comes up)
- Favorite Characters As Porn Stars
- …Literally hundreds more but I will save that for another book ☺

{Keep in mind that terminology has no say in what you arrive at the party as}

## <u>Body Raffle (or Swingers Raffle)</u>

This game can be played as a party game or with just two people. Feel free to make this as specific or as general as you would like. Perhaps one of the best aspects about this, is that is very simple and straight forward in its purpose as well as the way it is played.

- Get two decent sized containers. Depending on the number of people playing, they likely do not need to be that large.
- Get two sets of raffle tickets, which are available online or even at major retailers.
- Mark one of the containers "Names" and the other container "Acts" or something to the same effect.
- Write the names of each person participating on a raffle ticket. You can, of course, write each name more than once if you would like.
- On another set of raffle tickets, write one act (kiss, hug, oral, etc) per ticket.
- Place the names in one container and the acts in the other container.
- I'm sure you've guessed how it works; each person picks a name and an act from the containers. Obviously, in a heterosexual group, it's best to choose one gender to pick from the containers.

- Can also be used as a reward or punishment during another game.
- If it is just you and your significant other then it is always fun to use just one container filled with tickets with acts written upon them.  Place the container in a location that visitors would not disturb it.  Each day, pick something from the container that must be done.  With this sex life enhancement you would want to write specific acts with detail.
  - Example: Provide oral in the shower until you are begged to stop.  Do not tell them.

# <u>Balloon Keno the Naughty Way</u>

This game can be a lot of fun and despite the fact that it is a naughty game; it can make you feel like a kid again too, because of the popping of balloons. **Please, do make sure that no one around (not just participating) has any condition that would cause harm by sudden loud noises or the effects of balloons popping.** If a person nearby has such a condition, it is possible to tie the balloons in a way that allows them to be untied, or to clip them off well enough to hold the air in.

- Write anything and everything you can think of on little pieces of paper. Examples of things to write would be: articles of clothing, oral sex, streak around the room… just whatever you can come up with.
- Roll each little piece of paper and place them inside a dark colored unfilled balloon. One piece of paper per balloon.
- On most of the pieces of paper, write something such as "Bust" or even "lose a turn" and things that award you nothing.
- Blow up the balloons with the papers inside. There should be a rolled up piece of paper in each balloon, but only some should contain rewards.

- After all of the balloons have been inflated and tied or sealed in some way, write one number on each balloon. Be sure there are no duplicates.
- Now… scatter the balloons as best as you can in the playing area.
- Each player will guess a number and then pop the balloon with that particular number on it.
- Check the paper inside to see if you have won a reward.

---

- If it is impossible for those setting up the game, not to know which numbers would have  prizes in them… simply do not put numbers on the balloons…and instead, have each player pick from the stack of randomly scattered balloons.

# <u>Swinger Game Show</u>

As you can tell by the name this is a game for people who are swingers or open enough to go to extremes with anyone else in the group.  The concept and way to play is actually very simple though.

- Everyone of one gender (both if bisexual) stands behind a door or other large object that hides them fully.  The door they stand behind is chosen randomly.
- A player chooses a random door; winning the night or time with the person behind that door.
- This can also be done by having each person inside of different random rooms with the doors closed so the player can't see them.

As I said… very simple.

## Prank Wars for Roommates & Dorm Residents

Obviously, this game only works out if the roommates are of the right genders to want to see each other naked. If it is a college dorm hall that is playing… be careful for one, but again it would have to be a coed dorm. Unless everyone in the dorm hall happens to be gay or bisexual I suppose. You get the idea though I'm sure.

- Everyone knows what pranks are and most people know how to pull at least one or two on someone.
- The prank must be done IN THE RESIDENCE (Roommates must do it in the house they live and dorm hall residence must do it in the dorm hall) Pranks done outside of this area will not count in any way.
- If someone is caught by your prank, then they must flash something of the prank setter's choosing.
- You can use your imagination and take this to many other levels, but that will be left up to the players.
- Do not prank those who do not wish to participate.

- Be sure to not put anyone in danger and do not let the game get out of control.
- Step Up: If you are caught 3 times in one day by the same person = sexual favor.
- For clarification I will put this in here as well: If an entire group of people is caught by a single prank, then everyone in that group (who is playing) must flash something of the prank setter's choice.

# Naughty Who Done It?

This is live action roll play…with a very naughty twist. This is another game that is best suited for swingers or people with a similar lifestyle. Unless you tone it down, this game is pretty extreme; just to warn you. The good news is; this is also another game that is easy to understand how to play.

- One gender or team chooses a person, place, and weapon for a pretend murder. The suspect has to be someone that all players know or know of, but does not have to be another player.
- The opposite gender or team must do something naughty to or for each person of the first gender or team. The acts can go from flashing all the way to sexual acts. The entire group of players must decide before the start of the game.
- When the act or sexual favor is done, the person is given a clue by the one they did it for.
- Obviously a prize or reward must be thought of for the person to win once they have solved the mystery.

- Each person of the guessing team must go through and gather the clues. Once they have all gone through… and have the clues, they will have a set amount of time to solve it together.
- If they are unable to solve it within the time given, they can choose a punishment or they may opt to go through again and gather a second set of clues from each person of the opposite team.
- If you want to make this game more interesting… play at a party.
  - Do not establish an exact team.
  - Anyone who wants to guess… can.
  - They must flash any player they think may have a clue to solving the mystery.
  - A hint of how to find a clue holder must be given in some way, but not give it away easily.
  - This is more fun and daring because… they are bound to get it wrong and flash some lucky person at the party ☺

# Horny Zombie Attack
## a.k.a.
## Naughty House of Horrors

This is probably one of my favorite games that I have ever come up with…I must say. This one can get very funny as well as very sexy. You will need a house or private area in order to play. If you play in a field or something of that sort, be sure that you will not be disturbed… or you could get arrested. You've been warned ☺

- One of the greatest things about this game is that the scene or playing field can change each time you play if you are able to find areas that are acceptable and safe for playing.
- One player (can be more) must volunteer to be the "source" of the infection. Has to be a first zombie to start. Zombies are naked btw ☺
- Each player goes through the house or playing area. Must be a starting point and an end or exit point.
- If you are caught (touched) by the zombie, you must take off an article of clothing and then return to the start or entrance & go through again.

- Once you are naked… you are now infected and you become a zombie too. You must station yourself in the playing area and try to infect others.
- Everyone must go through until the last person makes it through without being infected fully. Last one standing kind of thing. That means that if you have on only underwear and every single other player is now a zombie…you must get all the way through without losing your underwear.
- Players are not left defenseless though. Spread through the game area by the first zombie should be weapons.
  - Can be containers (empty soda bottles work well) with paper saying what the weapon you have gotten is.
  - Can be any item that represents a weapon as long as everyone agrees on what it represents.
  - Things to have weapons do should be things such as:
  - * Blind a zombie of your choosing.
  - * A zombie of your choosing must crawl from now on.
  - * Vaccine found- gain immunity to one-time exposure (touched and stay clothed)

**Official Handbook for this game coming soon to Amazon & Kindle**

# Challenges/Bets That Are Great to Make

- Get a large bucket or container… fill it with water and place a quarter on the bottom. Challenge or bet someone that they can't pick up the quarter with using just their tongue. If they can then you will do something, if they can't then they must flash you (or whatever you come up with). If you want to make it more interesting…use beer instead of water. They will be drunk long before they get the quarter. If you use beer, you have to give the player goggles and ear plugs though because it can be harmful to your eyes and inner ear.

- Get three people. Tell them that you want all three of them to tell you what they did yesterday (a day they actually did things and didn't just sit around the house). Now, tell them that you want one of them to lie though. They get together and decide who the liar will be. Now, get them in a room one by one and have them tell you…but tell each one after they tell you…to tell it to you backward (last event first, first event last). The one that can't do it… or really stumbles…is lying.

# __Body Scape Races__

This is really fun and can be done two different ways really.  They are both equally fun though I must say ☺

- Two people lay down nude on a table, bed, or something…even the floor works.
- Put whip cream or any food that can be spread out on their bodies.  String it from the tops of their feet all the way up to the top of their neck (on the side of the neck).
- Two contestants must lick it from their person's body…the person who gets their person cleaned off first wins.
- This can also be played with just one person laying down nude.  Put a string of the food from the top of their feet all the way up to the top of their neck… put one string on each side of their body.  Then one contestant on each side of the person.  The trouble with this method is it is likely that the two contestants will keep bumping their heads together.

# Homemade Aqua Massage

A lot of people know about aqua massages that are offered at a lot of spas and rejuvenation places. It's very easy (and a little obvious really) to make one at home. It is obvious really, but most people simply don't think to do it. You know that taking a shower together can be very fun and erotic… this is another way to use the same shower.

- If you don't already have one, get a detachable sprayer for your shower. Be sure it has a spread out gentle setting, and a hard streaming setting.
- Warm the inside of the tub or set down a mat that is warm. Make sure that a person can slide on the mat easily though.
- Have the person sit with their knees up first.
- Massage them with your hand, while trailing the sprayer (at different settings) just above and over your hand.
- Repeat this process with them lying down as well.
- Great way to relax your partner as well as have some naughty fun… the slow touching and kneading of their skin; well into their deep tissue. For added fun… both of you get in the tub together and do this. Romantic:  you outside the tub and spoiling your partner though ☺

## FOR COUPLES

These are suggestions for 2 weeks. Start them any time and then each day you will check back and do what is written. Make sure you keep the days straight. This was born of a "Lovers Calendar" I created years ago and placed on a website I ran. Have fun...I'm sure you will ☺

### DAY 1

HIM: You must shave her pussy for her today, and then after you rinse her... use your tongue to check for stubble :-) Be sure you check everywhere and don't stop till she begs you for mercy from the pleasure.

HER:

You must tease him all day... be creative but don't hold back in your teasing... then get him off slow and strong, using only your hand.

### DAY 2

HIM:

Take her by the hair (you judge the roughness) and take her against the wall with her front pressed against the wall. Then bend her over the nearest piece of furniture and make her take it like you are angry at her. Don't ask...just do.

HER:

For the rest of the day, anytime he is sexual with you, you must call him "sir" or "daddy." When he is least expecting it... crawl to him on your hands and knees and beg him for what you want.

## DAY 3

HIM:

Once you've gotten her naked... bend her over your knee and spank her. Then finger fuck her hard while you have her there.

HER:

Picture message or email him naughty pictures while he is at work (or just away from the house). Be naked and waiting when he gets home. If need be... send him somewhere today to do this :-)

## DAY 4

HIM:

Get some oil (massage oil...preferably edible, baby oil, anything)... and give her an erotic massage, without trying to fuck her. You can always fuck her afterward, but make the massage last at least 30 minutes.

HER:

Lay him down and very slowly tease his body. Tease him all over and in every way you can think of. Make it good, but make him suffer before you bring him to an orgasm.

## DAY 5

HIM:

Tongue her asshole and finger fuck her while she is doing dishes, cooking, or laundry.

HER:

Suck his dick while he is on the phone today. Preferably with family and/or friends...not on a business call lol.

## DAY 6

HIM:

Make her beg before any penetration... all day!!

HER:

Take him in your ass at least once today including his entire load.

## DAY 7

HIM:

Do two household chores of her choosing, naked.

HER:
Whatever is cooked tonight must be served on your body... everything.  This includes any sauces, sides, and even the drink (make it wine to be more fun)... serve the drink down your leg and into his mouth or something of that sort.

## DAY 8
HIM:
Stroke one out slowly as you look at her nude body. (Best done while she does her task)
HER:
Sit him down and give him a strip tease.... once you are naked, straddle over him and masturbate to conclusion.  He is not allowed to touch.

## DAY 9
HIM:
In a shower together, you must wash her hair & after the shower lotion her whole body.
HER:
In a shower together, you must shave his dick & balls...then suck him off (or hand job)

## Day 10
HIM:
Before the day is thru, you must have gotten her off no less than 5 times with only your hand/fingers.

HER:

Lay on your back & putting the bottoms of your feet together; jerk him off (foot pussy) till he cums on your stomach/chest.

## DAY 11

HIM:

Let her blindfold you and spend no less than 1 hour exploring her nude body inch by inch. Pay attention to the sounds and wiggles she makes...learn all you can.

HER:

Sit him down in a chair with no arms naked. Tie his hands behind the back of the chair and tease him for as long as you'd like or he can stand.

## DAY 12

HIM:

Lay her down and sensually rub her feet... now kiss a line from the tops of her feet to just behind her ear. Good... now work your way back down. Then go back up but this time; go up just her inner thigh and stop when you hit something wet :-) Sure you can take it from there.

HER:

Tonight in the shower, stand behind him with your body pressed firmly against him. Reach around and use your hand to get him off. Now kneel in front of him and kiss all around his dick and balls (without touching them)

## DAY 13

HIM:

Write her several naughty notes/letters and leave them in places that only she will find them. By the end of the day... deliver all you have promised or mentioned.

HER:

Give him an oil show by oiling your body in front of him (editable massage oil is best to use) and then using your slippery body... titty fuck him to conclusion.

## DAY 14

HIS:

Tie her down on the bed, or standing to something over her head...now bring her to the edge at least three times before you let her cum.

HERS:

Make him cum (how is up to you)...now... tease and suck his dick before it has the chance to go down... don't stop until he begs you or he cums again.

# COUPLES CHALLENGES:

### COUPLE'S CHALLENGE:

Tonight you must "play" and make love wearing only a blind fold. Do not take the blind fold off (either of you) until you have BOTH cum hard.

### COUPLE'S CHALLENGE

Just Say Yes! Allow the other person to pick one sexual or naughty thing that can be done today/tonight...and you have to say yes to it. You both get at least one thing that the other person can't say no to.

### COUPLE'S CHALLENGE:

You 2 should get out more!! Drive (or walk) somewhere and have passionate sex either outside...or in the bathroom of a local business.

### COUPLE'S CHALLENGE:

Make love in every room of your house at least once before the day is over.

### COUPLE'S CHALLENGE:

Each of you write no less than 8 to 10 fantasies or role playing games that you would love to do (and are able to do today/tonight)... put them in a hat or bowl and mix them up on folded paper. Now... draw one or two out (depending on how much time you have)...and that is the one you must do.

## COUPLE'S CHALLENGE:

Call a friend and have them decide what position and how hard and fast you must have sex. Allow them to listen as you go at it if they want.

## COUPLE'S CHALLENGE:

You've used your hands enough today... both of you strip (or remain) naked...and play in every way you can but you are NOT allowed to use your hands in anyway.

## COUPLE'S CHALLENGE:

Fill the tub up with hot to warm water, so that the water stops about 6 inches from the top edge of the tub. Put whatever you'd like in it (bubbles, scents, etc). Play and make love without the water going over the edge.

## COUPLE'S CHALLENGE:

Easy one.... try at least two positions you have never tried before.

## COUPLE'S CHALLENGE:

Role Play one of these:
- Roman King & Servant-
- Roman Citizen & Slave-
- Roman Soldier & Enemy-
- Your Own Roman Themed Role Play-

## Other Titles Available:

"The Living Arc Angels"
"The Living Arc Angels Parental Version" (Safe for all readers)

** For announcements of new titles by Tim A Rowland, follow on Tumblr & Twitter **
TUMBLR:
http://authortimarowland.tumblr.com
TWITTER:
https://twitter.com/tim_a_rowland

OR Like on Facebook:
https://www.facebook.com/authortimrowland

# <u>NOTICE</u>

Have a naughty game, thought, or idea that you would like to share with the world?  Let me know by messaging me on Tumblr.  I plan to release a book filled with the ideas I like which are told to me from my readers.

You will be given full credit in the book.